G000270398

CRICKET
on the
VINE
1734-1984

CRICKET on the VINE
1734-1984

SEVENOAKS

"Thou, Vine, for pleasure and for sport designed,
Where lively activeness strings ev'ry nerve."

From Sevenoke By A. Harrod

K. J. SMART

with a foreword by E.W. Swanton

Photographs on pages 19 and 22, by courtesy of the Courtauld Institute of Art.

ISBN 0-9509141-0-X

Copyright © 1983 by Sevenoaks Vine Cricket Club

First Printed in Great Britain 1984.

Printed on Archive Text 160gsm
supplied by WWF Paper Sales UK Ltd.

Photoset in 11 on 12pt Palatino
by Rowland Phototypesetting Ltd
Bury St Edmunds, Suffolk

Printed and bound in Great Britain for
Sevenoaks Vine Cricket Club, Sevenoaks, Kent by
Biddles Ltd, Guildford, Surrey

Contents

Salute to the Vine by E. W. Swanton   6

Preface   8

In the Beginning   13

Between Two Wars   32

Cricket Under Fire   40

Into Modern Times   44

Salute to the Vine

by E W Swanton

A quarter of a century ago at Mr. Kenneth Smart's request I sent from Sydney – where I was following the fortunes of the MCC team of 1958/9 – an introduction to his essay on the ancient Sevenoaks Vine Cricket Club. I recalled playing in 1934 for MCC at the Vine in the week which celebrated the Bicentenary of the first recorded match at Sevenoaks. Now the score is creeping towards 250, and it is an honour as well as a pleasure to add these few words to as much of my former remarks as Mr. Smart in his editorial wisdom sees fit to retain.

Since I wrote last many developments have been duly chronicled by him, and in addition he has embellished his earlier story with the result of further researches. The important thing is that cricket continues to flourish in Sevenoaks generally and on the Vine not least. The School and the Club have even produced two more England cricketers to join J. Minshull, who played for England on the Vine in 1777. Lord Harris's History of Kent County Cricket Club tells us that Minshull scored 60 not out against Hambledon on that occasion, and describes him as being "as conceited as a wagtail". No one certainly can use such a phrase of either of his successors, Christopher Tavaré, our new Kent captain, and Paul Downton, son of George, who, alas and alack! was obliged after winning his Kent cap to obtain a Test place as a Middlesex cricketer.

I am pleased to note that the Vine more than holds its own in the Kent League; also that it continues to cater for its junior players and has now secured a ground at Otford to compensate for the loss of that formerly belonging to the Smithers family at Knockholt. With all this Mr. Smart, I can see, has had much to do. What a faithful and long-serving prop and stay he has been and still is – and how dependent clubs are on men of his calibre!

Nothing is more sure than that the earliest cricket matches were those contested by neighbouring parishes in the Weald. The villages of Kent and Sussex were the cradle of cricket and how far back those contests go is a matter which can never be exactly traced. The diarist of 1811 who records that the Duke family of Penshurst had been making cricket balls for the last 250 years may have been guilty of exaggeration; but he could equally have been perfectly correct. What we do know is that the popularity of cricket spread like a forest fire in the first half of the eighteenth century. It developed beyond the bounds of the countryside, to London, to the great schools, and to the Universities of Oxford and Cambridge. In Sevenoaks it had a firm and enduring foundation, under the patronage of the Sackvilles of Knole, "the greatest of all the feudal lords of cricket". It was a son of the first Duke of Dorset, Lord John Sackville, who made the critical catch in the historic game of 1744 at the Artillery Ground between Kent and All England, the score of which is the oldest surviving record of a match. The third Duke, who was one of the founders and promoters of MCC, was himself a good player, even if, as Mr. Altham remarks, the poet's enthusiasm outran both his judgment and his grammar when he wrote:–

> Equalled by few he plays with glee
> Nor peevish seeks for victory.
> His Grace for bowling cannot yield
> To none but Lumpy in the field.

Mr. Smart tells us about Lumpy, not to say Alfred Mynn, the record of whose accurate assault on his long-stop suggests the existence of a post-Regency Roy Webber. He presents to us the flourishing club of the present in the perspective of history, and he does so in order that the Sevenoaks cricketers of today and tomorrow may build worthily on an incomparable tradition. I have read his work with much interest and enjoyment. It is intriguing to follow the growth of a club from mediaeval beginnings, and it is even more pleasant to read of such present prosperity as is indicated by the turning out of five teams every week. A notion I particularly like is the award of the Club cap by the committee on grounds of merit. It is not enough to be a member. You must be a good member, which is not altogether the same thing. May I wish all fortune to the good and loyal members of Sevenoaks Vine, of whom the author of this history is assuredly not least.

E. W. SWANTON

Sandwich 1983

Preface

In reply to the many questions so often asked concerning the origins of cricket on Sevenoaks Vine, in 1959, at the request of the Committee, a short history was compiled in the hope that, as the years pass, future historians, spared the original research, will ensure that matters are kept up to date.

Over 20 more years of history have now passed and the notable events and people of that period have been put on record together with an expansion of the earlier sections so that this revised edition will coincide with the celebrations to mark the 250th Anniversary of the first recorded match at Sevenoaks.

Much help was received from the late G. B. Buckley author of "Fresh Light on 18th Century Cricket" whilst, in addition to the sources of information acknowledged in the text, I should mention H. T. Waghorn's "Dawn of Cricket" and "Some Notes on Sevenoaks Cricket and the Vine Cricket Ground" written in 1909 by J. S. Richardson, Captain of the Sevenoaks Club in the years preceding the First World War during which he was killed.

Although it has been possible to amplify Richardson's work in regard to the early years it is regretted that it has not been possible to answer the often repeated question as to how the Vine ground got its name.

It has been a pleasure and a privilege to undertake the necessary research to put on record the history of this famous Club which has given me so much fun and enjoyment during a membership of over 40 years as player and non-player.

K. J. S.

For 45 years Ken Smart has served Sevenoaks Vine Cricket Club as player, Committee member, historian and honorary groundsman.

After leaving Stationers School in Hornsey he joined Highgate C.C. but a family move to Kent in 1928 led to eleven successful seasons in London Club Cricket with Centymca.

Joining Sevenoaks Vine shortly before World War II he played constantly in the 1st XI until his 60th year and then adapted readily to the circumstances of village cricket for a few seasons in the lower sides.

Ken took over 1800 1st XI wickets for the Vine including three hat-tricks and a career best of 8 for 11 against Lloyds Bank in 1951. As a batsman he scored several hundreds and once shared in an opening stand of 220 with Fred Castle on the Vine where, on another occasion, coming in at number 11, he put on 110 in an undefeated partnership with Ron Terry for the last wicket.

Between 1934 and 1950 Ken played in several representative matches for the Club Cricket Conference and was awarded his cap in 1949 at the age of 38. After twenty years service on the Executive Council he was honoured with a Vice Presidency.

N. C.

In The Beginning

T he Vine at Sevenoaks is without doubt one of the oldest cricket grounds in existence, indeed an enquiry from the authorities at Lord's elicited the opinion that the oldest was one of three, Sevenoaks Vine, St. Albans or East Molesey.

The town of Sevenoaks has played a big part in the history of cricket since the beginning and the purpose of these notes is to set out the known facts in this connection as found in the records available to the Vine Cricket Club about the early times, followed by points of interest concerning players and events connected with the Club up to the present, so that future historians may continue from that point.

Much has been written about the possible relationship between earlier pastimes such as Cat and Dog, Cat-i-th-Hole, Rounders, Trap Ball, etc., and Cricket, but it is not possible to be dogmatic as to how the game really began. Probably it started in the downlands of Southern England with the target of the bowler being the entrance gate to the sheepfold known as a "wicket" which consisted of two forked uprights with a bar called a "bail" on top. Maybe the shepherd's crook was the earliest form of bat, being the forerunner of the curved implement of the 1700's.

From early references it can be deduced, with certainty, that a form of cricket was played in Tudor times and we also learn from a Royalist writer that in 1617 Oliver Cromwell, then 18 years of age, when in London "indulged in football, cricket, cudgelling and wrestling".

The first record of a cricket match appears in a court case resulting from the non-payment of a debt incurred from a wager on the match played at Coxheath on 29th May, 1646 between Samuel Filmer and Thomas Harlackenden on one side and Walter Francklyn, Richard Marsh, William Cooper and Robert Sanders on the other. The report of

13

the case can be found in the Maidstone Borough Records published in 1926.

Rev. James Pycroft author of "The Cricket Field", "Cricketana" and other books about the game, has written that in 1750 a writer, then 75 years of age, observed, "When I was a boy every cottage in the cricket playing districts in Kent had a well greased bat either kept in the bacon rack or hung up behind the kitchen door" and added that his grandfather was a famous local player in his day and "within these 10 years I could have shown you his name amongst a famous team preserved on a tablet over the chimney piece of the Inn at Sevenoaks".

Although, unfortunately, research has failed to reveal the name of the hostelry concerned, this is one of the most interesting references to the early history of cricket and its association with Sevenoaks.

Proof that the game was being played in the neighbourhood of Sevenoaks about 1610, is found in the Archaeologia Canteano, an annual publication of the Kent Archaeological Society.

In the report of a court case held on 12th May, 1640, concerning trespass at Chevening, it quotes information being given to the effect that "about 30 years ago there was a Cricketting between the Weald and Upland and this chalkehill distinguished".

The first written evidence of Sevenoaks playing a match is in the Grub Street Journal of 24th May, 1731, which refers to London playing Sevenoaks on Kennington Common a week later.

Another match between Sevenoaks and London, arranged for the 8th July, 1734, also on Kennington Common, did not take place, for, regrettably, Sevenoaks failed to appear and forfeited their deposit. (Whitehall Evening Post, 9th July, 1734.)

In the London Evening Post of the 10th September, 1734, there appeared a report of a match at Sevenoaks, played four days earlier, between the Gentlemen of Kent and Gentlemen of Sussex, whilst the Daily Gazetteer of the 18th August, 1739 gave notice of a game on the following Monday between Sevenoaks and Maidstone at Coxheath, twelve-a-side, for £500.

"We hear from Sevenoaks in Kent, that on Friday last an extraordinary Cricket Match was played there between the Gentlemen of Kent and Sussex. Lord Middlesex, Lord John Sackvill, etcetera, played for Kent, and Sir William Gage, etcetera for Sussex. The game ended to a very great Nicety in favour of the Kentish Gentlemen, but had so many diverting Turns in it, that the Lovers of that Diversion esteem it to be the best that has been played for many years. Yesterday the same Gentlemen were to play on the Downs near Lewes in Sussex but those that came down chiefly for Play have left this place in order to go for the Bath."

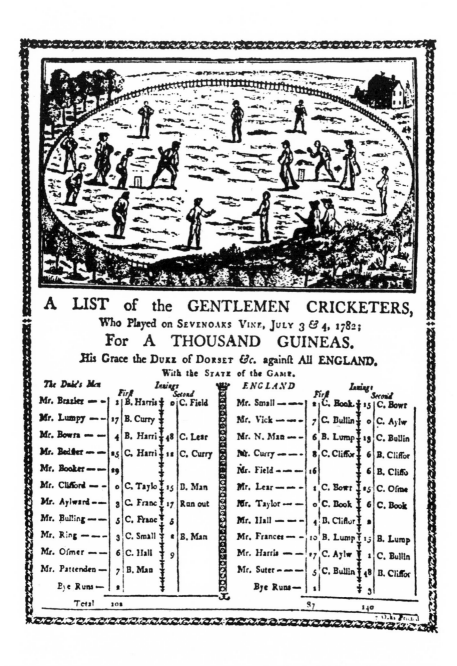

A LIST of the GENTLEMEN CRICKETERS,

Who Played on SEVENOAKS VINE, JULY 3 & 4, 1782;

For A THOUSAND GUINEAS.

His Grace the DUKE of DORSET &c. against All ENGLAND.

With the STATE of the GAME.

The Duke's Men	Innings First	Second		ENGLAND	Innings First	Second	
Mr. Brazier —	2	B. Harris	0 C. Field	Mr. Small —	2	C. Book	15 C. Bowr
Mr. Lumpy —	17	B. Curry		Mr. Vick —	7	C. Bullin	0 C. Aylw
Mr. Bowra —	4	B. Harri	48 C. Lear	Mr. N. Man —	6	B. Lump	13 C. Bullin
Mr. Bedster —	25	C. Harri	12 C. Curry	Mr. Curry —	8	C. Cliffor	6 B. Cliffor
Mr. Booker —	29			Mr. Field —	16		6 B. Cliffo
Mr. Clifford —	0	C. Taylo	15 D. Man	Mr. Lear —	1	C. Bowr	25 C. Osme
Mr. Aylward —	3	C. Franc	17 Run out	Mr. Taylor —	0	C. Book	6 C. Book
Mr. Bulling —	5	C. Franc	5	Mr. Hall —	4	B. Cliflor	2
Mr. Ring —	3	C. Small	2 B. Man	Mr. Frances —	10	B. Lump	15 B. Lump
Mr. Osmer —	6	C. Hall	9	Mr. Harris —	17	C. Aylw	1 C. Bullin
Mr. Pattenden —	7	B. Man		Mr. Suter —	5	C. Bullin	48 B. Cliffor
Bye Runs —	2			Bye Runs —	1		3
Total	**102**				**87**	**140**	

The Sevenoaks Vine staged many important matches in the Eighteenth Century.
a) Duke of Dorset's XI v All England July 3 and 4, 1782.

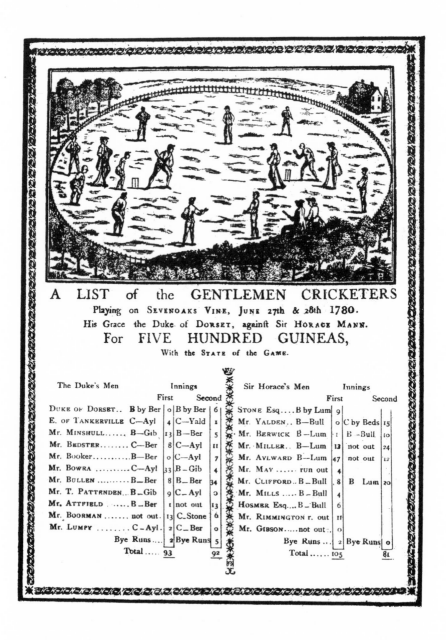

Wagers between great cricketing patrons were commonplace in the Eighteenth Century.
b) Duke of Dorset's XI v Sir Horace Mann's XI "for 500 guineas".

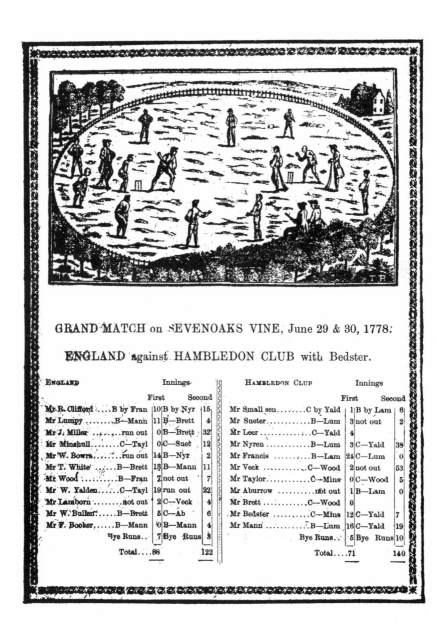

GRAND MATCH on SEVENOAKS VINE, June 29 & 30, 1778.

ENGLAND against HAMBLEDON CLUB with Bedster.

ENGLAND	Innings			HAMBLEDON CLUB	Innings	
	First	Second			First	Second
Mr R. Clifford ....B by Fran	10	B by Nyr	15	Mr Small sen........C by Yald	1	B by Lam	6
Mr Lumpy ....B—Mann	11	B—Brett	4	Mr Sueter............B—Lum	3	not out	2
Mr J. Miller ....run out	0	B—Brett	32	Mr Leer ....C—Yald	4	
Mr Minshull.........C—Tayl	0	C—Suet	12	Mr Nyren ....B—Lum	3	C—Yald	38
Mr W. Bowra........run out	14	B—Nyr	2	Mr Francis ....B—Lam	24	C—Lum	0
Mr T. White .....B—Brett	18	B—Mann	11	Mr Veck ....C—Wood	2	not out	53
Mr Wood ....B—Fran	7	not out	7	Mr Taylor...........C—Mins	0	C—Wood	5
Mr W. Yalden.....C—Tayl	19	run out	22	Mr Aburrow ....not out	1	B—Lam	0
Mr Lamborn ....not out	2	C—Veck	4	Mr Brett ....C—Wood	0	
Mr W. Bullen.....B—Brett	5	C—Ab	6	Mr Bedster ....C—Mins	12	C—Yald	7
Mr F. Booker,.....B—Mann	0	B—Mann	4	Mr Mann ....B—Lum	16	C—Yald	19
Bye Runs..	7	Bye Runs	3	Bye Runs..	5	Bye Runs	10
Total....	88		122	Total....71		140

This scorecard records the appearance of three Sevenoaks players Miller, Minshull and Bowra together in the England team.

From the History of Kent County Cricket by Lord Harris we learn that Sevenoaks played London on the Vine in 1740, and these two teams met again on the Vine on 23rd/24th August, 1743 in the first recorded match played over two days. The Kentish Gazette records that Sevenoaks beat Wrotham and Ightham by 56 runs, also on the Vine, on Wednesday, 1st August, 1772. Between that year and the end of the century many important games with more than local interest were played on this historic ground, such as:–

1773	Kent v. Surrey
1773	Hambledon with Yalden, v. England
1774	Kent v. Hambledon
1775	Kent v. Hambledon
1776	England v. Hambledon
1780	Duke of Dorset's XI v. Sir Horace Mann's XI for 500 guineas a side

It is on record in the Maidstone Journal that the match in 1773 between Hambledon with Yalden, and England was watched by 10,000 spectators. The full scores of this match are on display in the Vine pavilion.

England won by an innings and 51 and the Duke of Dorset, owner of Knole House, was included in their team. John Baker, an 18th century diarist who was present at the match, seemed impressed by the light hearted way in which Hambledon took their defeat. His entry on 29th June, 1773, includes the following:–

"The Hants crickets had one large room to themselves at the Crown Inn which is the Post Office and after each day, though so shamefully beat on each, spent the evening very merrily singing catches (and very well too) and some other songs with great joviality which made me a little doubt their being at all concerned."

The "Crown" Inn was doubtless the Royal Crown situated close to the Corner of South Park where the Post Office now stands. The hotel was demolished in 1932.

Organised club cricket as we know it today did not exist in the 18th century and the games were chiefly between different parishes usually for stakes. The teams would be composed of the gardeners, farm hands, huntsmen and foresters employed by the nobility and gentry under whose patronage the game prospered and grew. Some of the most notable of these feudal lords were the Sackvilles at Knole.

That there were attractions other than the cricket for spectators is revealed by this comment concerning a match early in the 18th century in the London Morning Advertiser at the time.

"The gentlemen who play in this match have subscribed for a Holland Smock of one guinea value which will be run for by two jolly wenches, one known by the name of the Little Bit of Blue, and the other, Black Bess.

They are to run in drawers only and there is excellent sport expected. Captain Vigers with a great many of his bruisers and bull dogs will attend to make a ring."

18

John Frederick Sackville, Third Duke of Dorset (1745–1799)
A portrait by Sir Joshua Reynolds
(Reproduced by kind permission of Lord Sackville).

The Penny London Morning Advertiser of 24th June, 1748, reports another race following the cricket match on Walworth Common between High Kent and the Black Swan Club.

> "The contestants, Mary Weaver of the Borough and Sarah Lucas from Rotherhithe, this time ran stark naked."

The game at that time was, of course, quite different from today. For instance, the bowling was all underarm along the ground and to combat this the bat was shaped like a hockey stick. At first the wicket was two feet wide and one foot high consisting of two stumps and a bail. Later, although two stumps and one bail were still used, the wicket was heightened to 22 inches and narrowed to 6 inches.

The batsman was not out unless the bail fell to the ground and the frequency with which the ball passed through the stumps without dislodging the bail led to the introduction of a third stump to which reference is made later in these notes.

Before the introduction of the popping crease to replace the original "popping hole" between the stumps, runs were made by the batsmen touching the bats held by the umpires. This necessitated the "square leg" umpire standing near the wicket in the short leg position and this custom was continued for some time after the need for it had been removed.

Winning the toss gave choice not only of innings, but also of the pitch, which had to be "within 30 yards of a centre determined by the adversaries" and the selection of the pitch was usually left to the leading bowler.

The change from parish to club cricket was, no doubt, gradual and from the information available it is not possible to say exactly when the change took place in Sevenoaks.

Lillywhite in his preface to "Scores and Biographies" gives the date of the formation of the Sevenoaks Vine Club as 1750 or 1760, whilst F. Richards in his book "Old Sevenoaks", published in 1901, says that "the old Vine Club was formed late in the 18th century". We do know, however, from the Kentish Gazette, that a meeting of the Sevenoaks Club took place on the Vine on the 15th May, 1788.

Meetings about this time apparently took place on Thursdays, and the first record of the names of those attending is on 22nd June, 1797. The Maidstone Journal gives the following:–

Sir J. D. Dyke, Bart.	Capt. P. H. Dyke
Sir W. Geary	Richard Allnutt, Esq.
Sir Richard Glode	Rev. Mr. Morton
W. Evelyn, Esq.	Rev. M. Walter
John Mumford, Esq.	P. Nouaille, Esq.

The earliest Sevenoaks Club matches of which we possess the full scores, are those with East Malling in 1800, and Homerton in 1802, whilst in the Annals and Scores of the West Kent Cricket Club we have complete details of the regular fixtures between Sevenoaks and West Kent from 1817 to 1831. The Napoleonic Wars caused a temporary decline in cricket and the Sevenoaks Vine Club became dormant for 17 years. It was resuscitated in 1848 by Capt. W. B. Northey and in 1850 was granted a two day fixture with MCC at Lords which was lost by 103 runs, Sevenoaks Vine scoring 80 and 61 against the MCC's 85 and 159.

In a three day match scheduled for 6th–8th September, 1841, the first and only attempt was made to enclose the Vine ground and charge for admission (6d.) when Sevenoaks with five of England met Tunbridge Wells with five of Kent, including the famous Fuller Pilch and Alfred Mynn. We are told that the venture was not wholly successful. Alfred Mynn was of course, the renowned Kent fast bowler who was said, on one occasion, to have struck long stop on the chest with six consecutive deliveries so that he had to be taken home, and spat blood for a fortnight!

According to the Sevenoaks Advertiser of October, 1841, rain fell so heavily on the second morning that play had to be suspended after Tunbridge Wells had been dismissed for 44 including 10 wides. The writer goes on to say:–

"In the latter part of the afternoon, however, the weather cleared up a little but to the great disappointment of those who had assembled to witness the game, the Tunbridge Wells gentlemen could nowhere be found to resume their stations."

The Vine ground has not always been in the fine condition in which it is kept today (entirely at the club's expense), and because of its poor state it was abandoned in 1875. At the invitation of the Amherst family,

Earliest known photograph of the Vine Ground, Sevenoaks.
Vine versus Harrow 5th September, 1858.

Amos Pett, G. Hooper, A. Bartholomew, C. Allworth outside Pett's shop where
Freeman, Hardy and Willis is now.

21

who were largely responsible for the management of the Sevenoaks Vine Club at that time, matches were played at Montreal Park. A return to the Vine was made the following year. In 1877 the Sevenoaks Vine CC absorbed another club then in existence called Sevenoaks, and between 1878 and 1881 a large sum was spent on levelling the north west corner of the Vine, the work being carried out by Amos Pett, one of the famous family of bat makers, who had a shop at 121 High Street, Sevenoaks. In recognition of his work, the club, strangely enough, presented him with a bat which is now exhibited in the pavilion. In 1897 another move was made, this time to Lord Hillingdon's home at Wildernesse, (now Dorton House) where matches were played until 1910 when the Sevenoaks Vine Club became dormant for a second time. The Captain of the Vine

Edward "Lumpy" Stevens
A portrait by Almond painted in 1783
(Reproduced by kind permission of Lord Sackville).

Club whilst at Wildernesse was the heir to Lord Hillingdon, Hon. C. Mills, who was killed in the First World War.

Some idea of the behaviour of Vine pitches about this time may be gained from the following extract from a report in a local paper of a match during Cricket Week in 1896:–

"Carr was especially effective on Wednesday and his fast deliveries on a hard wicket (a gentleman who has something like cosmopolitan experience described it as disgraceful) rendered things extremely unpleasant for the Mote. Bruises and contusions were distributed among them with amazing impartiality whilst, unfortunately, one or two of the visitors sustained serious injury."

In 1898 a club named Sevenoaks Town took over the Vine ground and in the following year the word "Town" was dropped thus bringing into existence once again a club called Sevenoaks, with Herbert Laurie acting as both Captain and Secretary for several years.

The Minutes of the Sevenoaks Club give some idea of the difficulties experienced at this time in trying to improve the condition of the Vine ground. After Sam Apted, the head groundsman at the Oval, had been called upon in 1898 to undertake some levelling and other work on the square at a cost of £50 and to give his advice, large amounts of marl, loam and manure were spread on the turf not to mention the Sevenoaks Council's sweepings off the streets.

Between 1898 and 1903, four different groundsmen were employed until some stability was reached when J. Grayley took on the job and held it for fourteen seasons. The weekly wage paid makes interesting reading, viz 30/–d. in 1898, reduced to 24/–d. in 1902, raised to 27/6d. in 1903 and 28/6d. on the appointment of Grayley.

Sevenoaks continued to play on the Vine until the outbreak of the First World War in 1914, when the ground was taken over by the military as a parade ground, and saw no cricket for four years.

Thus ended an era in Sevenoaks cricket, one which had seen several important developments in the game itself. Originally, scores were kept by cutting notches on sticks but in 1776, the first known score cards were printed by Pratt, scorer to the Sevenoaks Vine Club. The early underarm bowlers had changed their style from along the ground, to pitching a length, and this had caused the hockey shaped bat to give way to the upright type.

Then in 1835, it was made legal for the bowling arm to be raised as far as the shoulder, and 29 years later the bowler was given the full freedom of action as enjoyed today.

Another interesting change was the introduction of the third stump, brought about following the famous single wicket match in 1775 between 5 of Hambledon and 5 of England on the Royal Artillery ground at Finsbury, when Lumpy Stevens, the England bowler who was employed at Knole, bowled several balls through the two stumps without dislodging the bail.

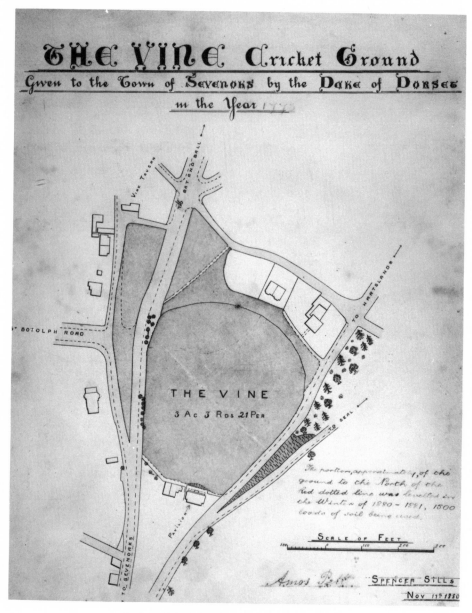

A plan of the Vine Ground, Sevenoaks 1880.

The following interesting extract from the diary of Richard Hayes of Cobham, Kent, shows that two stumps were still being used in important games in 1776:–

"26th June, 1776. I set off about seven in the morning to Sevenoaks Vine to see Hambledon play with All England at cricket. The Duke of Dorset bowled ye first four balls. Not a run got, but soon took to hitting. Hambledon got 241 runs. The Duke made two remarkably good catches. The Duke was bowled out after getting six runs. I heard him say if he missed a ball he was sure to be out. The Hambledon men were in between five and six hours. They beat us in guarding their wickets and in standing out too. N.B. They talk of having three stumps. By their playing with very broad bats and playing all ye blocking short play, so that it is a very hard matter to hit a wicket. The Hambledon men beat All England by getting as many runs in one innings nearly as all ditto did in both their innings."

The actual scores of this game were Hambledon 241 and 84, England 173 and 77.

H. T. Waghorn in "Cricket Scores, Notes, etc., from 1730–1773" states that the first reference to the use of three stumps in a match is in the Kentish Gazette of 4th June, 1777, where the following appears:–

"On Sevenoaks Vine on Wednesday, 18th June instant will be played the first match for a thousand guineas, Hambledon (with the Rt. Hon. Earl Tankerville) against All England. The wickets to be pitched at ten-o-clock and to be played with three stumps to shorten the game."

In the event, however, Hambledon made 403, a very high total for those days, of which Aylward scored 167, a feat described by Nyren as "one of the greatest feats upon record in the annals of cricket" seeing that it was done against Lumpy Stevens regarded as the finest bowler of his day. Aylward is said to have gone in at 5 o'clock on Wednesday and was not out until 3.00 p.m. on Friday.

About 1773, the Vine ground was given by the 3rd Duke of Dorset, owner of Knole and a great patron of the game, to be a cricket ground for ever and to him the town of Sevenoaks owes a great debt.

An interesting record survives of a match on the Vine in June, 1766 in which the Duke of Dorset was involved, in the form of two bills which read as follows:–

11th June, 1766
Wine delivered to His Grace of Dorset's booth by Benjamin Dransfield:–

	£	s	d
1 dozen of Red Port	1	4	0
10 bottles of White Port	1	0	0
To the use of decanters, glasses, etc. and attendance		2	6

His Grace the Duke of Dorset bought of Wm Pett 1766			
12th June Eleven Cricket Batts	1	7	6
20th June 1766 Rec'd the Contents			

For Father Wm Pett
p Thos Pett

It was in 1850 that the pavilion was built for the Countess of Amherst who let it to the Cricket Club. Before this, use had been made of the "Cricketing House" which was later turned into two cottages which were demolished to make way for the erection of the bandstand in 1894. The pavilion was bought in 1890 by the Sevenoaks Urban District Council who allowed the use of it free of charge to the Cricket Club, the latter being required to pay the rates and taxes and to be responsible for internal repairs and maintenance.

During the period under review, one of the Sevenoaks players, Joseph Miller, a gamekeeper to the 3rd Duke of Dorset, appeared for England, scoring 73 v. Hambledon on the Vine in 1773. Among the many who played for Kent were the 3rd Duke of Dorset himself; William Bowra, another gamekeeper at Knole; the Rev. W. W. Rashleigh, a master at Tonbridge School, and later Vicar of Horton Kirby who appeared in 98 County games between 1885 and 1891 and G. M. Kelson who played 69 times between 1859 and 1893, and in 1864, was chosen for the Gentlemen v. Players at the Oval.

The "Cricketing House" as it was known, was used by players on the Vine before the erection of the pavilion in 1850. The house was demolished to make way for the bandstand which now stands on the site.

Opening of the Bandstand August, 1894.

Two others who should be mentioned are Viscount Holmesdale, who was president of the Kent County Club in 1861, and Amos Bartholomew, who was groundsman and umpire to the Vine Club for 30 years. It is reported that "once with rare pluck he fought a navvy who tried to assert his independence by damaging the turf on the Vine and after a severe conflict thoroughly vanquished him." Vandalism on the Vine is obviously no modern phenomenon.

Two local cricketing licensees were T. Sewell, who came to the Chequers in 1849, and Thomas, junior, who kept the Railway Tavern. The former played for Kent in 1852 and for the Gentlemen from 1839–47, whilst his son assisted Kent from 1856–66 and was a member in 1861 of the first team of England cricketers to play in Australia. The tour was sponsored by Spiers and Pond.

Other interesting personalities to be Vine playing members, were Cardinal Manning (1825) who became Roman Catholic Archbishop of Westminster, and Sir William Hart Dyke, MP (1857), one time owner of Lullingstone Castle, who became President of the MCC in 1880. He is reputed to have bowled probably the widest ball yet seen on the Vine, for, according to the Annals of the West Kent Cricket Club, "it cut over point".

Married versus Single on Sevenoaks Vine, 1880.

Heaven forbid that such a thing should happen today, but in the late 1820's the Vine were accused by some of their opponents of having a twelfth man on their side in the person of umpire Berwick (nicknamed "upon Tweed"), who was just over 5ft. in height and wore a blue coat with brass buttons, reaching to his heels. His build was portly and it is said that when a bowler who was being incommoded, asked him to stand sideways, he replied, "Lord Sir, I be bigger that way!"

In 1848 any member joining the club paid an entrance fee of 5s.0d. and a weekly subscription of 3d. all the year round. A certain amount of discipline seems to have been exercised at that time, for any member not reporting for practice at 7.00 p.m. on Wednesdays was fined 2d., and anyone selected for a match had to pay 2s.6d. if failing to give three days' notice to the Secretary, of his inability to play. The Committee met weekly in summer and monthly in winter, and a payment of 1s.0d. was required from anyone missing more than two meetings in succession.

Of the relics in the possession of the Club, one is a bat of the type used in the earliest days and autographed by Richard Mitchell in 1745. It was presented by J. S. Killick, CBE in 1932. There is also one made by William Pett the famous bat maker about 1755 and sold for 4/6d.

Another interesting item is a silver snuff box in the form of a cricket ball marked with seams, which dates from 1818. It is said to have been tossed from hand to hand at the Club Dinner which was, in those days, held in the afternoon, also on other convivial occasions, and anyone dropping it was fined a bottle of wine or half a crown.

The original snuff box is kept at the bank but a replica, kindly donated by P. E. Leach in 1965, is always on view.

Kent's last inter-county match on the Vine was against Sussex on 10th/11th August, 1829. Present day spectators whose only pleasure is to see the bowlers hit for six or four should spare a thought for those who watched a meeting between the same counties two years earlier when T. Pierpoint, in his second innings for Sussex, scored 31 in 7½ hours!

Some idea of the social attitudes and habits of the mid-nineteenth century, as well as the respect in which the playing strength of the Sevenoaks Vine CC was held, may be gained from quotations from two letters addressed to Mr. G. Carnell, then the Hon. Secretary of Sevenoaks Vine CC

In one dated 12th August, 1851, a Mr. Bradley Norton of Town Malling CC says:–

"I am desired by the Committee to decline your kind challenge as the greater part of our players are farmers and sportsmen and cannot make it convenient to play during the shooting season."

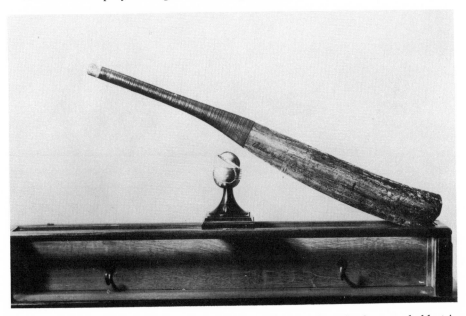

This bat autographed by Richard Mitchell in 1745 is thought to be the second oldest in existence. It was presented to the Sevenoaks Vine Club by J. S. Killick CBE in 1932. Also shown is the silver snuff box in the shape of a cricket ball which came into the Club's possession in 1818.

CORONATION

OF HER MOST GRACIOUS MAJESTY

Queen Victoria.

THE
Sevenoaks Festival
In honour of the event will take place (and no mistake)

ON WEDNESDAY next, July 11th, 1838.

The spirited Inhabitants of the far famed Town of SEVENOAKS having raised a *separate* fund and appropriated the amount to FIREWORKS and FUN, the following unrivalled attractions and amusements will take place (time permitting); and in the arrangement of the pastimes the Committee intend doing *all* that can be done, and (on this particular occasion) something *more*, trusting to a generous Public for approbation.

Pearls of Poesy presented to the Parish Peasant Population.

Roast beef and plum pudding with "out and out" cooking,
Invite you (most welcome) on Wednesday to look in.
The fun and the revels take place on the Vine;
The "firework brigade" go on duty at nine.
Don't come without tickets*—to caution attend,
Or perhaps you'll return without "pitcher or friend."
Then haste to the festival joyous and gay—
Glad faces—good appetites—"**nothing's to pay.**"

* These Tickets are limited to the Inhabitants of Sevenoaks, and are now all distributed.

Contention up the Pole for a Leg of Mutton.

Young aspirants have now the opportunity afforded them of occupying a high station in the world, and it is hoped no one will be so *sheepish* as to decline to "lift a leg" on this occasion. The soap is warranted of the softest quality, and has no affinity to sand or saw-dust. All candidates' pockets will be examined previous to their ascent, with a view to detecting smuggled ammunition.

A JINGLING MATCH

(Twelve Men to play) for 20 minutes for Four Shillings. The Jingler (if caught) to receive Two Shillings.

A CORONATION GOWN

To be run for by Sixteen Girls under 20 years of age. The second Girl to receive a tasty

VICTORIA CAP.

The victorious fair one will have the opportunity of selecting from the most approved patterns, a Gown piece (of 6s. value), which may be the envy of the Village. The Cap (of 3s. value) may be set at the young men as soon as possible.

An Interesting Little Pig

Will be introduced in the ring, and offer his tail to the notice of Competitors. This animal has been selected from a large family in the vicinity, for its beautiful tail and dulcet notes; it is hoped it will not be deemed a *bore* to attempt its capture.

25 Yards of PRIME CALICO.

This prize having already been before the public, and under their plates at dinner requires no further comment. Calico may be applied to various purposes, and those who have been accustomed to make *shifts*, may now wear *shirts*, and stick up a collar with their neighbours. **To be Run for by Twelve Men.**

A BRAN NEW HAT

For the successful candidate from Ten persons, at
Whipping the Ball from the Hole.

Candidates who enter the List will be allowed to "cut and come again."

TWELVE DONKEYS

To be ridden by Boys, no Boy to ride his own donkey, the *last* is to be declared the winner,
To Race for 4s. The second Donkey (the rider is meant) to receive 2s.

TWELVE MEN TO JUMP
100 Yards in Sacks, for 6s.

Each man to provide his own sack, which must not exceed four bushels. The second man to receive 3s.
In this Race it is feared several Candidates will "get the sack," and that only.

A RACE WITH TWO JUMPS,

(12 Men to start,) for FOUR SHILLINGS and a WELCH WIG.

It is earnestly requested by the Committee, that in the event of any competitor falling in this race he will not stop to get up again; and all parties starting are at liberty to jump as high above the fixed bar as they please, and as wide as they choose.

4 Boys to climb Greased Ropes

for a pair of splendid CORDEROY BREECHES, with highly-gilt Buttons.
These Breeches will be fitted to the successful boy on the following day, in order that no *breaches* of decorum may take place on the course.

TWELVE MEN, BLINDFOLDED,
TO RACE WITH WHEELBARROWS,

100 Yards for a LEG OF MUTTON, and a TAM O'SHANTER. Each man to come provided with his own wheelbarrow.
These circumventing navigators in wheel (weal) there is little doubt will feel the luxury of whoa (woe). It is particularly urged that the competitors take great care of their shins.

Expected to be showy, but not fast. Number unlimited. Each Jockey to ride his own donkey with his (not the donkey's) face to his tail. A piece of ordnance will be fired to start these "Jerusalem Tits."

A DONKEY RACE,

(Banging Ascott and Epsom hollow) by Boys, for FOUR SHILLINGS, and a RED NIGHTCAP; open to "Bits of blood, bone, and muscle" of all ages.

The Members of the Jockey Club intend being present; and betting to extensive amounts has taken place. The foreign Ambassadors have orders to purchase the winner (between them) at any price. The successful Jockey will be expected to subscribe a "Joey" towards the St. Leger next year.

††† This Race will come off (perhaps the rider too) from Barrack corner up the road to a flag post to be placed on the Vine. The company are requested to form themselves into a Donkey Police to keep the course clear, and prevent accidents during this race.
Application for the entry for the Races to be made to Mr. VINCER, *Chemist*, Seven Oaks, not later than 2 o'Clock on Tuesday the 10th instant, and the Committee will decide upon the persons who are to be entered by drawing lots; the decision may be known on application to Mr. VINCER, on Wednesday morning at 10 o'Clock.
No person can be admitted on the course except the Committee, their Agents, and several of Her Majesty's "Beef-eaters," who will keep the ground.

The above Amusements will end with a

Grand Rural Country Dance
ON THE VINE;

On which occasion the splendid green carpet (supplied by Dame Nature) will be allowed to remain, and the Company are requested not to open the windows for fear the ladies might suffer from other draughts (*than Beer*. White Kid Gloves and Pumps will not be admitted. It is confidently reported in the **Parish** circles that Mr. T*******s********n will lead off with the much admired and lovely Miss L************************.

A piece of ordnance will be fired to announce the time for Dancing.

A FIRE BALLOON

(Rude Boreas permitting)

Will ascend during the afternoon, and any person desirous of having a bird's-eye view of the festive scene, and joining some choice spirits into the "regions of space" may be accommodated on payment of Two hundred Guineas. An early application can alone secure a seat in the car, which from necessity will be too small to be visible to the naked eye at starting. And at NINE o'Clock in the Evening precisely, a most splendid, unequalled, never-to-be-surpassed, and ever-to-be-remembered

DISPLAY of FIREWORKS

Will take place under the immediate superintendence of the celebrated J. C. D'ERNST, Artist in Fireworks to Her Majesty, The Royal Gardens, Vauxhall, London, and every where else besides.

God save the Queen, and bless her People!

Programme for the Sevenoaks Festival on the Vine in 1838 to mark the Coronation of Queen Victoria.

The other, dated 27th August, 1851, is from Mr. E. Chapman of Tunbridge Wells CC in which it is stated:–

"According to my promise I have spoken to several of the cricketers here as well as the Gentlemen players to get up a match with Sevenoaks but the feeling is that the players here have no chance and they therefore wish to decline."

Some light on what local cricketers wore during the 19th century is given by a writer who states that in 1901 there were residents in Sevenoaks who could remember when it was considered "infra dig" for a player to go on the Vine unless properly attired "in a high hat and Wellington boots".

Before concluding this review of the early years there is another event of historic interest to record. On 31st August, 1769, J. Minshull scored 107 for the Duke of Dorset's XI v. Wrotham on the Vine.

This is the first recorded individual hundred and the fact that each batsmen's scores are known shows that scoring in this game cannot have been on notch sticks.

Minshull, who as mentioned earlier played for England, was employed as a gardener at Knole at a weekly wage of 8/–d. but was dismissed in 1772 with a month's notice. Apparently, he had charged his employer, the Duke of Dorset, 3/10d. for a bushel of potatoes and 1/–d. each for 54 pots of carnations which had been produced on the Estate!

He was described by Richard Nyren the famous cricket writer as "a capital hitter and a sure guard of his wicket and was also conceited as a wagtail".

During this period before World War I, the two lowest scores on the Vine yet recorded were the 18 by Sevenoaks Vine v. West Kent on 4th June, 1877 and 14 by West Kent on 21st July, 1891 in reply to Sevenoaks Vine's 301–5 dec.

On 4th June, 1910, J. D. Adamson made 211 for Sevenoaks, the highest individual score yet recorded on the Vine but most of his runs were scored after a result to the match had been obtained.

Between Two Wars

f rom 1914–18 the Vine had been used by the Army for drill and also for football. The seating in front of the pavilion was roofed over and the building used as a canteen by the YMCA. who also had a hut on the ground.

When they left they took with them the Cricket Club's tables, chairs and even the clock, and as Army units stationed in the neighbourhood, "forgot" to return all the tackle they had borrowed, the club, in 1919, possessed nothing.

The ground was in an appalling condition quite unfit for cricket but thanks to the work of R. N. Marchant the newly appointed groundsman, it was possible to re-start fully in 1920, after playing three games in 1919.

Due mainly to the efforts of H. T. Cross and T. A. Grose, the Vine CC returned from Wildernesse to play on the Vine and, for a second time, an amalgamation took place with the Sevenoaks Club, resurrecting the title Sevenoaks Vine CC in 1921.

Club cricket flourished during this post-war period and although rebuilding was somewhat slow at first, Sevenoaks Vine in a few years regained its rightful place as one of the leading clubs in Southern England with a strong and attractive fixture list.

One game played in 1922 against West Kent at Chislehurst is worthy of mention. The Vine declared at 302 for 5 leaving their opponents 2¼ hours to get the runs. It may be hard to believe but the records show that they did so with 5 wickets and 15 minutes to spare!

By the early 1930's Sevenoaks Vine were fielding four sides each Saturday, the Whole Day and Half Day teams using the Vine ground while the other elevens played away or on Knole Paddock which was then available to the club throughout the season.

This photograph taken in 1919 shows the YMCA notice on the pavilion which was used as a canteen for the troops training on the Vine during the 1914–18 war.

The five day week was not common then as it later became and, in consequence, the Whole Day side was often changed so that the Half Day or 2nd XI was at times the stronger combination.

Many fine players appeared for the Vine in the inter-war years and they cannot, of course, all be named. Among those who will long be remembered, however, are H. J. Taylor, a first class batsman who played for Kent several times, G. D. Durtnell one of the most prolific and attractive batsmen in the club's history and S. G. Smith a highly competitive all rounder.

Their deeds together with those of many other fine players such as T. A. Grose, C. W. French and R. N. Marchant are recorded in the score books of the period, which are among the club's treasured possessions.

Ron Marchant the groundsman, was a capable all rounder who specialised as a right arm medium pace bowler and slip fielder and was also an excellent coach. It is interesting to remember that in the 1920's and 30's several clubs refused to renew fixtures with the Vine unless they agreed to omit him as a professional from their team! Net practices at that time were held from 4.00 to 8.00 p.m. and Marchant was present each day as "Ground Bowler" to bowl to members who required his services.

H. T. Cross captained the club immediately after the war, to be followed by Herbert Thompson for 8 years and Geoffrey Durtnell for 6 years. D. C. G. (Gordon) Raikes took over in 1937 and held the office

33

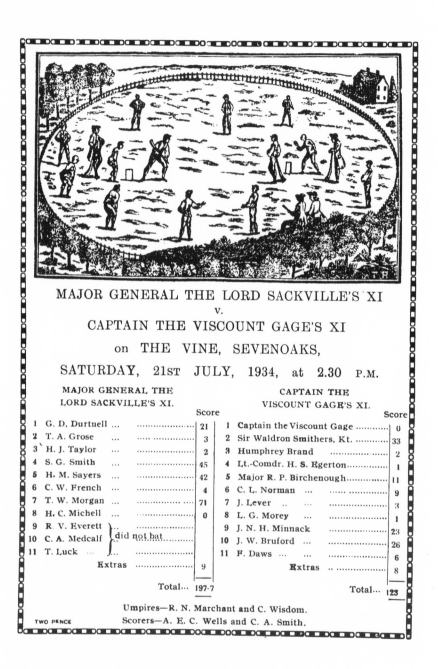

MAJOR GENERAL THE LORD SACKVILLE'S XI
v.
CAPTAIN THE VISCOUNT GAGE'S XI

on THE VINE, SEVENOAKS,

SATURDAY, 21ST JULY, 1934, at 2.30 P.M.

MAJOR GENERAL THE LORD SACKVILLE'S XI.	Score		CAPTAIN THE VISCOUNT GAGE'S XI.	Score
1 G. D. Durtnell ...	21		1 Captain the Viscount Gage	0
2 T. A. Grose ...	3		2 Sir Waldron Smithers, Kt.	33
3 H. J. Taylor ...	2		3 Humphrey Brand	2
4 S. G. Smith ...	45		4 Lt.-Comdr. H. S. Egerton	1
5 H. M. Sayers ...	42		5 Major R. P. Birchenough	11
6 C. W. French ...	4		6 C. L. Norman ...	9
7 T. W. Morgan ...	71		7 J. Lever	3
8 H. C. Michell ...	0		8 L. G. Morey ...	1
9 R. V. Everett			9 J. N. H. Minnack	23
10 C. A. Medcalf } did not bat			10 J. W. Bruford ...	26
11 T. Luck ...			11 F. Daws	6
Extras	9		Extras ...	8
Total...	197-7		Total...	123

Umpires—R. N. Marchant and C. Wisdom.
Scorers—A. E. C. Wells and C. A. Smith.

TWO PENCE

The scorecard of the 1934 Bicentenary match was a clever replica of the sort used by Pratt in the Eighteenth Century.

34

until after the 2nd World War. Raikes who gained a blue at Oxford in 1932 kept wicket for Gloucestershire in the following year.

In 1934 the Bi-Centenary was celebrated on the Vine, of the match played at Sevenoaks in 1734 between the Gentlemen of Kent and the Gentlemen of Sussex. This game, staged in the costume of the period, gained much publicity in the Press. The original Deeds of the Vine ground have never been found and so, during the Bi-Centenary festivities, Lord Sackville took the opportunity of confirming the gift of his famous ancestor. Later an agreement was drawn up, under the terms of which the Club are required, on demand, to pay two peppercorns per annum, one for the ground and the other for the pavilion, to the Local Authority who, in turn, must pay, when asked by Lord Sackville or his successors, one cricket ball within the wicket gate of Knole on the 21st day of July in each year.

An appeal was launched at this time to raise money, to replace the pavilion with a brick structure, but as the sum received was insufficient the existing building was extended and reconstructed internally. At the same time a new scoring box, with moving figures, was erected at the east end of the pavilion. This box, which in modified form is in use today, was generously presented by D. C. G. Raikes and replaced what had been described in the local press as "a little stained wooden box of unsightly appearance and entirely out of keeping with the design and colour of the pavilion".

The two elevens, umpires and "notchers" posing for a photograph before the Bicentenary Match of July 1934.

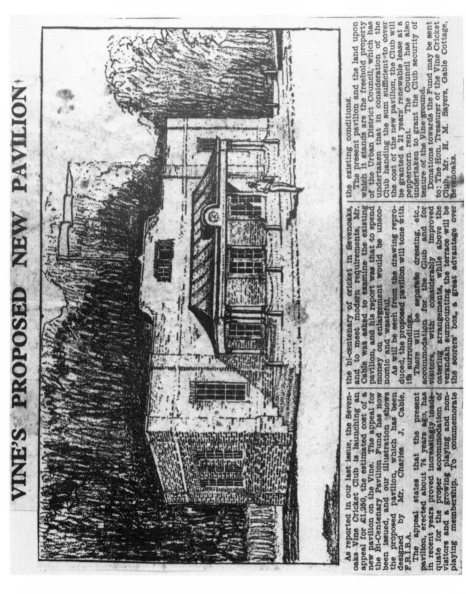

VINE'S PROPOSED NEW PAVILION

As reported in our last issue, the Sevenoaks Vine Cricket Club is launching an appeal for £1,260, the estimated cost of a new pavilion on the Vine. The appeal for the Bi-Centenary Pavilion Fund has now been issued, and our illustration shows the proposed pavilion, which has been designed by Mr. Charles J. Cable, F.R.I.B.A.

The appeal states that the present pavilion, erected about 74 years ago, has in recent years proved increasingly inadequate for the proper accommodation of visitors and a growing playing and non-playing membership. To commemorate the bi-centenary of cricket in Sevenoaks, and to meet modern requirements, Mr. Cable was asked to examine the existing pavilion, and his report was that to spend money on enlargement would be uneconomic and wasteful.

As will be seen from the drawing reproduced, the proposed pavilion will tone with its surroundings.

There will be separate dressing, etc., accommodation for the Club and for visitors, with considerably improved catering arrangements, while above the verandah surmounting the terrace will be the scorers' box, a great advantage over the existing conditions.

The present pavilion and the land upon which it stands are the freehold property of the Urban District Council, which has undertaken that in consideration of the Club handing the sum sufficient to cover the cost of the new pavilion, the Club will be granted a 21 years' renewable lease at a peppercorn rent. The Council has also undertaken to grant the Club security of tenure of the Vine ground.

Donations towards the Fund may be sent to: The Hon. Treasurer of the Vine Cricket Club, Mr. H. M. Sayers, Gable Cottage, Sevenoaks.

A new pavilion on the Vine as proposed in 1934. The plan was abandoned when the appeal failed to reach its target of £1,250.

This photograph shows the new scorebox presented by D. C. G. Raikes in 1936.

Members of the Bicentenary Match elevens outside Blighs Hotel in Sevenoaks High Street.

Members of the Bicentenary elevens photographed in London Road, Sevenoaks.

Gordon Raikes leads out the Vine versus the late B. H. Valentine's XI on 24th April 1937. Also in the picture are Geoffrey Durtnell of the old established Brasted firm of builders (third from left) and R. J. Rogers (third from right), the Cudham schoolmaster killed in an air raid on Biggin Hill in 1940.

Another much appreciated gift was made by G. D. Durtnell in the form of coloured glass leaded windows for the bar with their attractive cricket motif. The reconstructed pavilion was officially opened by Lord Sackville in April, 1937.

G. D. Durtnell

1938 saw the laying of two concrete practice pitches at the south west corner of the Vine. These were widened about 15 years later, and one was subsequently removed in 1962 to provide more space for a grass practice area.

When the 1939 season opened, the shadow of another World War was drawing ever nearer and when, at the beginning of September, the blow fell, cricket on the Vine came to a sudden end for the season. The heavy air attacks which were expected at once did not, however, materialise until a year later, and some clubs in the district restarted after a week or so, one of them at Cudham playing a match as late as November, in which several Vine players took part.

Cricket Under fire

Unlike 1914–18, club cricket continued throughout the 2nd World War although, of course, on a limited scale and the Vine Club kept going without a break apart from the few weeks immediately following the outbreak of war when the pavilion was commandeered for the use of evacuees, and again a year later in September, 1940, at the height of the Battle of Britain, after several games in August had been interrupted by air attacks on local airfields, necessitating players and spectators seeking shelter.

Between the middle of June and the end of September, 1944, a number of the matches were played with V1 flying bombs, known as "doodle bugs" passing overhead on their terrifying mission to London and its suburbs.

In one instance the engine of one of these missiles cut out as it came over the Vine pavilion in the middle of an over. Immediately, players and umpires threw themselves flat on the grass in anticipation of the coming explosion. Miraculously, however, the engine started up again and the bomb continued on its evil way.

In typically English fashion everyone rose to his feet without a word and the match continued as if nothing had occurred.

Although during the nightly blitz on London in October, 1940 a bomb destroyed the Club Hall, situated on what is now part of the Vine gardens, and a parachute mine hit Walthamstow Hall, the Vine ground and pavilion escaped damage apart from some broken windows.

For two seasons it was possible to field two sides each week but from 1942–45 one team only could be raised. A few of the leading players were usually available and with members on leave filling some of the places, the Vine were usually able to provide a good game for all their opponents. These regularly included Buccaneers, Linden Park, Orping-

40

ton and Tunbridge Wells, whilst other fixtures were with the Leicester-shire Regt. Stationed at Wrotham, Royal Army Pay Corps captained by W. A. Hill, who led the Vine 2nd XI after the War for several years, Bromley Police who included S. G. Smith of Vine fame, and various Service units stationed in the locality. Mention should here be made of H. W. Pearce of Otford who could always raise a side when a fixture was wanted, and did much to keep cricket alive in the district at the time.

That the Club was kept going was due in large measure to the enthusiasm and hard work put in by C. T. Butler, the Secretary, E. A. Tootal, Treasurer, and R. S. Ash, the Match Secretary and Vice Captain to D. C. G. Raikes, who was able to play only occasionally.

Rarely, if ever, had the Vine had two centuries scored against them in the same innings until on 8th May, 1940, they visited Tonbridge School who that year were represented by one of their best ever elevens. For the school in a total of 222 for 5 dec'd T. R. Wood contributed 103 and R. A. Smith 102. In reply the visitors were dismissed for 179, several of their wickets being taken by the late Geoffrey Sims who subsequently became a much respected member of the Club. Sadly more than half the school team were shortly killed serving in the Royal Air Force.

On 24th August, 1940, F. J. Castle (129), the Knockholt schoolmaster who later played for Somerset before losing an eye in a cycling accident, and K. J. Smart (120) scored 220 for the first wicket against Haileybury, this being the highest opening partnership for the Club, on the Vine, yet recorded.

The Vine scored 347 for 2 in this all day match but an afternoon air raid caused delay and the match was drawn with the visitors scoring 176 for 7.

Strangely enough, the very next week, when Richmond Public Schools were the visitors, their opening pair, M. J. Cassy and C. C. Russell Vick, who became Vice Captain of the Vine 1st XI in 1956, made an even bigger stand, putting on 253 before being parted, in a game which was interrupted five times while players and spectators took shelter during air attacks on Biggin Hill airfield, in the basement of Sennocke Engineering Company – now the Stormont building.

On 11th July, 1945, playing at home against an RAF XI, Sevenoaks Vine had lost 9 wickets for 112. Coming in at Number 11, K. J. Smart joined R. H. Terry and these two remained together until the innings was declared closed at 222 for 9. There is no record of any higher partnership for the last wicket being scored on the Vine.

With R. N. Marchant becoming Local Education Welfare Officer in 1942 and petrol being severely rationed, ground maintenance became a big problem. G. D. Baker, who was employed at a local petrol station and unconnected with the club, ensured that the motor mower was kept in use and due to his efforts the outfield was maintained in excellent condition.

Frank Ashdown, well known as a local umpire for many years, prepared the pitch each week. Ashdown, then advanced in age, had,

The only photograph taken of Vine cricket during World War II. Sevenoaks Vine versus Southborough on the Vine 19th August, 1944.

L to R. *A. Holmes, G. L. Brown, J. Collis, J. Parkin, F. Paige, T. Farmar, F. Ashdown, E. A. Tootal, N. C. Watson, R. N. Marchant, K. J. Smart, R. S. Ash, A. Basil-Jones, H. Pearce, G. Durtnell, J. S. Lark, G. E. Turner, W. R. Cleveley, P. A. Cullen, M. Goulden.*

however, very little previous knowledge of the work and by the beginning of 1945, with the end of the war in sight, the state of the square had greatly deteriorated.

In an effort to get the ground into good condition for the members who would soon be returning from the Forces, a Ground Committee of R. N. Marchant, J. Robinson and K. J. Smart was formed and, under the expert guidance of the first named, they prepared the pitches and worked on the square whenever they were able to do so.

Thus the situation was saved in time for the resumption of normal post-war cricket in 1946.

Just as hostilities in Europe were ending in May, 1945 there arrived on the scene Percy Acres a former Army Band Sergeant who for the next twenty years until his death in November, 1964, rendered quite outstanding service as first eleven scorer. Spurning anything slipshod, each winter quite voluntarily he transferred the playing records of all the teams into one book applicable to the season just ended. These books remain on view in the pavilion as a lasting memorial to his devoted service to the club of which he was so proud to be a member.

P. C. Acres

A memorial plaque on the pavilion wall records the names of playing members who lost their lives on active service in both World Wars. Included is that of R. J. Rogers, the Headmaster of Jail Lane School at Cudham who, with his wife, was killed in their garden shelter at Biggin Hill by one of our own anti-aircraft shells.

The names on the plaque are:–

1914–18
G. H. Heslop, T. Sillis, J. S. Richardson, C. C. Theobald

1939–45
S. H. Cotton, D. Morgan, F. H. Moss, R. J. Rogers, J. S. Tootal,
L. C. Martin, T. Morgan, C. Neve, D. Smithers, A. D. Pain

Regrettably the name of the Hon. C. Mills referred to earlier was omitted from the list of those killed in the 1914–18 war.

Into ModernTimes

n January, 1946, W. J. Fairservice, the former Kent County player,
was given a 5 year contract as groundsman for 8 months in each
year with coaching Club members as part of his professional
duties.

Although 23 years had passed since he last played for the County, his
arrival at Sevenoaks with its attendant publicity, helped to attract many
new members, both playing and non-playing, and made a significant
contribution to rebuilding and expanding Club activities at a most
important time.

Fairservice was, however, 65 years of age when he came and with
advancing years taking their toll his enthusiasm for the work began to
wane. On one occasion he left a telephone message for the Captain that
the Vine was unfit for the match due to be played there that evening.

In view of the limited amount of rain which had fallen on Sevenoaks
that day the puzzled Captain decided to go and make his own inspec-
tion. To his surprise he found one end of the pitch dry and the rest very
wet. The mystery was solved by a local resident who reported having
seen Fairservice proceeding to and from the pavilion with a watering
can. Evidently he had failed to complete his self imposed task. His
contract was ended by mutual consent with a year to run.

He was succeeded in 1950 by J. R. Bonnett who came straight from 25
years employment with W. A. Franks the ironmongers in the High
Street. Like his brother George, one time gardener to Sir Rudyard
Kipling, who succeeded him after 16 years, he had no experience of
work on cricket grounds but under the tuition of Ron Marchant who had
become the Chairman of the Ground Committee, both quickly learnt the
job, and rendered good, faithful service.

M. Begent   *W. J. Fairservice*

Following the retirement of George Bonnett in 1970, the club has been served by a number of groundsmen for short periods in D. B. Rolleston (1 year), L. Blakely (1 year), P. Clarke (5 years). In 1979 Ian Haffenden, a playing member, was appointed, but left the district after one season and was succeeded by Bill Roxburgh, another with no previous experience of pitch preparation, who accepted guidance from K. J. Smart.

The immediate post-war years brought widespread enthusiasm for cricket throughout the country and Sevenoaks Vine certainly enjoyed its share. With a rapid increase in membership and large numbers watching the home matches, the Club flourished and grew, until in 1955, five teams were being fielded each week. By 1957 it was sometimes possible to put out six. The 1st XI did not resume whole day Saturday cricket in 1946 but decided to start matches at 2.00p.m. thus enabling the strongest available side to be fielded each week.

For four seasons following the war the Club possessed in Maurice Begent an exceptionally accomplished batsman and cover point who seemed destined for the highest honours. As a teenager he had achieved outstanding success with Orpington, before joining the Vine. He was offered a contract by Kent which he declined and then, soon after his marriage, he gave up the game at the very early age of 26 to the dismay of the many to whom his prowess had given so much pleasure.

In 1949, his last season, the 1st XI was possibly as strong and well balanced as it has ever been and a writer on club cricket in a London Weekly Sports Journal at this time, named Sevenoaks Vine, jointly with two other clubs, as the best of the season. He added:

> "They get their award because of their fighting spirit, the general overall quality of their play, great batsmanship, good length bowling, accurate fielding and for their general conduct and bearing on and off the field."

The annual Cricket Week, which had been a notable feature in the life of the town between the wars, was revived in 1946, but whereas it had formerly been held in July, it was moved to the first week in August. For year after year it was plagued by bad weather and in desperation, advice was sought from the Meteorological Office. This having elicited the fact that records over many years showed that the beginning of August was notorious for bad weather in the South East of England, the week was moved, in 1972, to the end of August with much better fortune. In 1977 it was again changed, this time back to its original date in July.

For many years Cricket Week created great local interest, many people taking a week's holiday to come and watch. With the main streets being decorated and the shops running a window dressing competition with a cricket theme, a real festive atmosphere was created.

Regrettably, however, interest in the Week by the public greatly declined, and all the former sense of occasion has gone. The introduction of sponsorship of some of the games by local businesses in the late 70's was a mild but welcome stimulant.

From 1955 to 1981, it was possible to run a second Cricket Week, early in the season, for the benefit of members of the teams below the 2nd XI who play all their Saturday matches away from the Vine. This was abandoned in 1982 for a tour in the West of England.

To assist the large number of spectators then attending matches on the Vine, by announcing details, enabling them to follow the play more

R. B. Divall

46

closely, a microphone, amplifier and loudspeaker were installed in the pavilion in 1948. These were used for several years until, in the late fifties, television and widespread ownership of the motor car caused a marked change in social habits, resulting in a large drop in the numbers of those watching cricket on the Vine.

In the spring of 1956 an appeal was launched for £1,000 for the reconstruction of the interior of the pavilion, to give more space, to extend the building on the east side, and to put a balcony over the score box. The response was most generous, and the sum was raised in about 6 months, enabling the work to be completed by the opening of the 1957 season. P. E. Leach, a Club member was the Architect.

The balcony provided a magnificent view of the cricket but, unfortunately, the ills which seem to beset flat roofs brought its use to a speedy end.

An interesting event also took place in 1956 when Lord Sackville asked for the cricket ball due to him from the Council, who, in turn, requested the Vine CC to pay to them the peppercorn rents for the ground and pavilion. The ceremonies at Knole House and on the ground were televised and broadcast by the BBC. Other opportunities for widespread publicity for the Club during this era were provided first by the BBC, when in 1947, J. G. Sagar was interviewed by the late Richard Dimbleby in front of the pavilion in the "Down Your Way" programme, and then in 1962 by Independent Television when K. J. Smart took part in a live feature on Sevenoaks and spoke of the Club's history and showed some of its relics.

Paying the Rent.

One cricket ball being handed by Councillor Robinson to Lord Sackville, "within the wicket gate" at Knole when the ceremony was filmed by the BBC during Cricket Week in 1957.

This unfinished painting by Rex Divall, a Vine player, was found among his possessions after his death aged 32 in 1966.

During the first ten years or so after the 1939–45 war, a number of special matches were played on the Vine by outside organisations e.g. some Kent 2nd XI games, the Club Cricket Conference v MCC and several Women's fixtures under the auspices of the Women's Cricket Association including Kent v The Australian Women's Touring XI in 1951.

A short official film of this game is now preserved on behalf of Sevenoaks Vine Cricket Club in the National Film Archives by the British Film Institute in London.

In 1948, coaching in the Vine nets was organised for young players between 14 and 18 from other clubs and local schools, who did not normally have access to facilities essential for their proper development. This was carried out by some of the Vine's senior players and resulted in the discovery of Alan Morris, then 15 years old, who later joined the Vine and developed into a very gifted performer.

Having abandoned this scheme, it was decided in 1952 to concentrate on developing the Vine's own youthful talent by forming a Junior Section and playing matches during the school holidays. This has continued for many years and has developed into a very important part of Club activities, its organisation owing much to the hard work of a few devoted members and their wives!

In 1949 a Club Cap was designed in Navy Blue with a silver badge – the colours of the old Sevenoaks Club who played on the Vine in the years immediately preceding the 1st World War. This Cap can only be worn by those to whom it is awarded by the Committee. Playing ability is not the only qualification, loyalty and service rendered play a big part.

A maroon tie with silver emblem to be worn by playing and non-playing members was introduced in 1951, also a flag in the same colours.

Another interesting event at that time was the transfer by the then Sevenoaks Urban District Council of the summerhouse from the garden of Solefield House to the north west boundary of the Vine for use as a tea hut for spectators, at a cost of £158.

D. C. G. Raikes gave up the Captaincy of the Club in 1950 after 13 years in office and was succeeded by N. P. Golds whose consistency as a right hand batsman brought him a great number of runs in his own individual style, including 3 centuries in successive innings in 1948.

Norman Golds was a particularly lucky spinner of the coin and in 1952 he won the toss on 22 occasions in 35 matches. Invariably he chose to take first innings and the powerful batting at his disposal usually led to a big score, which opponents, anxious to show that they had avoided

D. C. G. Raikes

N. Golds

defeat at the hands of the Vine, were loth to chase, with the result that 17 games were drawn. This led to some rather unjust criticism of the Vine Captain for negative play, by a local clergyman in a letter to the Sevenoaks press, and, following the entry of the Club's Hon. Press Representative into the discussion, in defence of his Captain, some lively and interesting correspondence ensued.

H. J. Francis

A. F. E. (Ted) Collins

If nothing else, this served to demonstrate the interest there was at this time in the cricket on the Vine and how many people in the town identified themselves with their local Club.

J. B. Parkin, who succeeded Golds in 1953, had the distinction of having led the 4th, 2nd and 1st XIs and it was during his term of office that A. F. E. (Ted) Collins arrived on the 1st XI scene. During a season or two in the 2nd XI his medium pace left hand bowling had met with only moderate success but with the departure of N. L. Gavin, the 1st XI's slow left armer, to Catford Wanderers, Collins decided upon a complete change of style.

It quickly became clear that he had the precious gift of deceptive flight and winning Gavin's place in the 1st team he met with quite outstanding success. In six seasons (excluding any Sunday play), he took 640 wickets and on 6th September 1958, against Bromley on the Vine, he claimed 5 victims in as many balls. His total of wickets for that season was 132.

Beset with a problem of weight which he failed to overcome, he left the cricketing scene as suddenly as he arrived but his name must surely feature in any history of the Vine Club.

Another who left his mark about this time was F. R. Axten, a talented and aggressive batsman and a fine fielder who, on 8th August, 1959, during Cricket Week scored 189 v Gore Court on the Vine. His innings, which included 23 boundaries and 3 sixes, is the highest innings so far recorded for the Vine whilst a match was still "alive". Reference has already been made to Adamson's 211 in 1910 much of it coming after a result had been obtained.

F. R. Axten

In 1956 Club leadership passed to G. C. Downton, first choice wicket keeper for the Club Cricket Conference for many years. George had previously been with Orpington and played several times for Kent in 1948 when Godfrey Evans was on Test duty. D. C. G. Raikes, the Vine wicket keeper before Downton's arrival, had, as previously mentioned, played for Gloucestershire in 1933 and he also appeared in a few games for Kent in 1948.

A. E. Morris, an attractive, attacking left handed batsman, a product of the original coaching scheme for boys in 1948, became Captain of the Club in 1962 for two years and was followed by D. J. Preston who had played for Sussex as an all rounder for two seasons in the late '50s.

It was in July, 1962 that Morris (123) and Preston (100), scored 226 for 0 against Kings School at Canterbury, which is the highest opening stand yet recorded for the Vine in an away match. Morris declared at this total and the Vine achieved the doubtful distinction of being defeated without having lost a wicket!

Morris also featured in another notable partnership in 1965 when he and George Downton scored 265 for the second wicket against Tunbridge Wells on the Nevill ground.

With the arrival in 1961 of Alan Hurd, an off spinner with county experience with Essex, to join Derek Preston, slow left hand, the Vine had, for several years, probably the most formidable spin attack in Club cricket. Hurd succeeded to the Captaincy in 1967.

51

About this time, a number of the Vine's long serving players had retired, among them K. J. Smart, a member of the 1st XI since the late 1930's. It could well be some time before his tally of more than 1800 1st XI wickets is passed.

Schoolmaster Alan Hurd was in charge of cricket at Sevenoaks School and this happy association ensured that most of the School's outstanding cricketers found their way to the Vine. Two of these who subsequently achieved distinction with Kent were Chris Tavaré, a batsman of the highest class who first played for England in 1980 and Paul Downton (son of G. C.) who was selected as reserve wicket keeper in

Two first class wicketkeepers, George Downton and his son Paul, together in the Vine 1st XI in a Kent League match at Dover on 6th September, 1975.

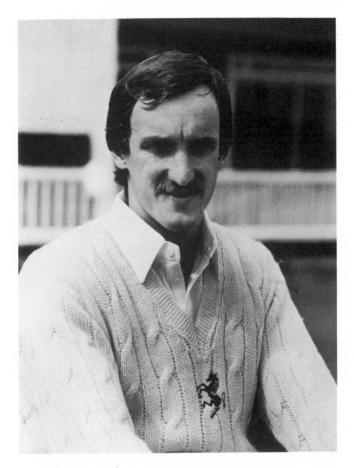

C. J. TAVARÉ
Sevenoaks School, Sevenoaks Vine, Kent and England

the England party which toured Pakistan and New Zealand in 1977/78 and gained his cap for England in the Test series in the West Indies in 1981, after leaving Kent for Middlesex. He thus became the fifth Sevenoaks player so far to appear in an England side.

1970 ushered in a decade which saw several important changes. In 1948 a meeting of the representatives of Sevenoaks and District clubs at the Miners Arms in Dunton Green, had rejected a call to form a local league, although as a result of this same meeting the Sevenoaks branch of the Association of Kent Cricket Clubs came into being.

Furthermore, the Club Cricket Conference to which Sevenoaks Vine, together with more than 2,000 other clubs, belonged, had, since 1915 as one of its main objects "the fostering of amateur cricket on a non-competitive basis". It was therefore against League Cricket, which of course, had flourished in the north of England for many years.

Now, however, at the instigation of the Surrey County Club, a suggestion was made in public by Raman Subba Row, the former England batsman, that a trial should be given to League Cricket in the South.

Very soon leagues were being formed all over the Home Counties and beyond, so that it rapidly became a case of a club joining a league or being faced with great difficulty in arranging fixtures.

The Club Cricket Conference was, therefore, forced to change course and its aim is now curtailed to read, "to foster amateur cricket".

The Vine speedily adapted themselves to the new situation and, joining the Kent League in 1971, became champions in the following year, repeating this success in 1978, on both occasions under the leadership of R. N. Golds, son of a former Captain, N. P. Golds. In 1979, they finished as runners up under W. Gray, a master of Sevenoaks School, who had succeeded to the Captaincy. He, in turn, was followed in 1982 by R. Herkes who had had county experience with Middlesex.

Kent League Champions in 1978.

J. Scholfield, S. Beaumont, G. Spelman, A. Sims, P. Edwards, M. Benson, I. Haffenden, J. Hornsby, R. Golds, G. Downton, I. Walker.

This aerial view of the Vine ground shows the hockey pitch at the northern end. Hockey has been played here since 1967.

Although the league game, with its limited overs and emphasis at times on containment rather than the dismissal of opponents, was not to the liking of many, there is no doubt it brought about a big improvement in fielding and under Golds the Vine 1st XI became quite outstanding in this department of the game.

For some years the Sevenoaks Hockey Club had been granted the use of the Vine ground and pavilion during the winter by the Cricket Club but at an Extraordinary AGM in July 1973, a merger of the two clubs into the Sevenoaks Vine Club with Cricket and Hockey sections, was agreed upon. Some of the Cricket Club members had misgivings as to the outcome of this union but financially and socially, at least, it could be termed a success.

In 1975/76 primarily to meet the needs of the Hockey section, a substantial extension to the pavilion on the west side, with major improvements to the interior of the existing building was carried out. The cost in the region of £35,000 was raised in 7 months including grants and loans. P. E. Leach was again the Architect.

Many regretted that, of this large sum, nothing was spent at the time on the cricket score box which was in urgent need of modernisation and repair.

Work in progress on the extension to the pavilion carried out in 1975.

In keeping with modern trends, 1978 saw the introduction of sponsorship for the matches in Cricket Week, local business firms taking responsibility for one day each.

Inevitably sponsorship spread to the League fixtures and this led to an extraordinary situation arising on the Vine on 21st July, 1979, when Sevenoaks Vine 2nd XI were playing Bromley 2nd's in the 2nd Division of the Kent League. As the game was about to start, it was found that the sponsor's name was not on the ball provided, and 40 minutes were lost before play started, while a ball bearing the desired maker's name was located some miles away and brought to the ground.

Another change had taken place in 1970 when, after protracted discussion and consideration of all aspects of the matter, it was decided to start playing some limited Sunday cricket on the Vine. For some years Sunday home matches had been played on the Club's other ground at

Knockholt which, with its peaceful rural situation and relaxing atmosphere was ideally suited to the Sunday game.

It was in 1957 that, with the demise of the old Knockholt Club, Mr. Norman Smithers had granted the Vine CC the use of his beautiful ground at Homefield, Knockholt, free of charge, provided that they maintained it in good order at their own expense. It was a relic of the old days of country house cricket and during the Vine's tenure it was made into a first class playing arena which lacked only adequate pavilion facilities. For some time the Club were much indebted to a member, D. P. Winter, for looking after the ground, and then for a number of years after his retirement from business in 1969, K. J. Smart gave many hours of loving care in an effort to provide a good playing standard for the members in the 3rd, 4th and 5th XIs who had to play their home matches away from the Vine, and for the Acorns on the Sunday. It was a sad day for him as, of course, for the whole club when all this came to an unhappy end.

In September, 1976, Mr. Smithers died and the ground subsequently was bought by a Mr. Komedera, a Polish millionaire. He refused all pleas to sell or rent the ground and denied the Vine CC the right to play there after the 1978 summer. This created serious problems in trying to find alternative venues for about 40 home games in a season, including Junior Section matches in the school holidays which had previously been played at Knockholt. One result of this was the severe curtailment of home fixtures for Sevenoaks and District Wednesday CC who have provided mid-week cricket in Sevenoaks since 1900 and had been privileged to play all their home games on the Vine.

At this point it is appropriate to record that between 1937 and 1971, Sevenoaks Wednesday had, in Arthur Hammond, one of the most consistently successful batsmen in local cricket. His record of 16,500 runs on Wednesday afternoons only, including 29 centuries, with an average of 50.50 speaks for itself.

The summer of 1976 will be remembered for the great drought, when hardly a drop of rain fell in the Sevenoaks area during the cricket season until mid-September. With a local ban on the use of hose pipes, without legal backing as it turned out, water had to be purchased and brought to the Vine by tanker from the Marley lake at Riverhead.

Inevitably, there was a deterioration in the state of the pitches and the season was curtailed so that the square could be re-sown. Some of the fixtures were transferred to the ground at Knockholt where there was no prohibition of the use of hoses and the green oasis there in the middle of a brown desert of a field, was a source of amazement and some envy to visiting teams.

A four year search for a ground to replace Knockholt ended successfully early in 1982 when land was purchased at Otford. Planning permission for change of use from agriculture to sport was, at first, refused, but a subsequent appeal was successful.

Due to much hard and dedicated work by John Hilder, planned and

During the great drought in 1976 water was brought by tanker from the Marley lake at Riverhead to keep the cricket square on the Vine alive.

The former summer house at Solefields Lodge was moved by Sevenoaks Council to the north west corner of the Vine in 1951 for use as a tea hut for spectators.

organised by Jack Parkin, one of the longest serving Club members, astonishing progress was made enabling the ground to be ready for the first Hockey match to be played there on 15th January, 1983.

By the end of the following May it was found that a limited amount of cricket would be possible during the 1983 season and the cricket square was used for the first time on 19th June on the occasion of the Kent League Six a Side competition.

At this stage there were no changing facilities of any sort available on the ground and following the efforts made in purchasing the land, the fulfilment of plans to provide a permanent pavilion will test to the full the enthusiasm and determination of all concerned.

By those outside, a club is judged by its 1st XI and understandably much has been written in these notes of the activities of the premier team.

There must however, be no overlooking all those who make up the 2nd, 3rd, 4th and 5th and Junior teams including umpires and scorers who have played their part over the years in keeping this famous Club in the forefront, together with those devoted Club members, sometimes, alas, too few in number, who, although maybe not distinguished players, have done so much behind the scenes to keep things going and to help create enjoyment and pleasure for others on the field. Long may they continue to be found, so that whoever it may be in years to come, has the task of bringing this history up to date, may have a continuing story of success and prosperity to record.

Extract from a poem "Sevenoke", Humbly inscribed to His Grace the Duke of Dorset, by A. Harrod, 1753.

> Thou, Vine, for pleasure and for sport design'd,
> Where lively activeness strings ev'ry nerve;
> What lofty hills encompass thee around!
> See the selected spritely bands advance,
> Big with the hope of Conquest, and of Fame.
> From nervous arm, with force impulsive, see
> The crimson ball attack the destin'd mark,
> The Youth's disastrous, short-liv'd, luckless chance
> Prompts his successor to avenge his cause.
> Quick from the repercussive bat aloft
> The mounting ball divides the yielding air.
> Th' advent'rous Youth, with eager eye intent,
> And nimble feet, springs o'er the shaven plain,
> Her airy course pursuing. Far o'er head
> She takes her lofty flight, his speed avoids,
> His pains evades, and downwards furious darts
> With sudden haste, swift gliding on the green.
> The war grows high; shouts echo o'er the plain,
> And ev'ry breast, ambitious, pants for Conquest.
> Again the ranks renew'd, the harden'd ball
> Flies, with its usual vigor, to the goal.
> Again repuls'd, she soars; ah, luckless chance!
> Just where the watchful Youth stops her career,
> And ere she kiss the ground, he grasps her fast.
> Around the circle shrill applauses ring,
> Sent up to Heav'n in acclamations loud.
> The rural Lass, with cheeks like ruddy morn,
> And joy extatic, sees her wish confirm'd.
> She flushes crimson transport and delight;
> Soft pleasing pleasure pants within her breast,
> And in her eye her Lover stands reveal'd.
> As Fortune smiles or frowns, their hopes and fears
> Alternately prevail. Anon the Victors
> Full flush'd with Conquest, and elate with Joy,
> From social bowls quaff deep the potent juice.
> 'Tis now the Vanquish'd find returning vigor:
> Th' exhilarating liquor fires their breasts;
> And emulation runs thro' ev'ry vein—
> Altho' repuls'd, they scarcely own they're conquer'd,
> And to another onset dare the foe.

In the Schweppes Bicentenary Competition open to all clubs of 200 years of age, Sevenoaks Vine were judged by David Frith, Editor of Wisden Cricket Monthly to have the most fascinating history. On behalf of the Club, Nigel Cannon received the prize of a Schweppes Bicentenary Plate and a cheque for £250 from England Cricket Captain Bob Willis

A working party of Club members helping to change the new ground at OTFORD from agriculture to sport. 1982

Sevenoaks Vine Cricket Club Dinner, Royal Crown Hotel, Sevenoaks 1931

Sevenoaks Vine Acorns XI which took part in the last match on the Knockholt ground on 1st October 1978